FOLK SONGS OF SCANDINAVIA

Folk Songs from Denmark, Finland, Norway and Sweden
For String Orchestra, Violin Groups or String Quartet
Arranged by KITTY PÄÄKKÖNEN

Violin 1

Violin 2

Viola

Cello

Bass

Violin 3 (Viola t.c.)

Piano/Conductor Score

Art Layout: LISA GREENE MANE

© 2001 Summy-Birchard Music
division of Summy-Birchard Inc.
All Rights Reserved   Printed in USA

Summy-Birchard Inc.
exclusively distributed by
Warner Bros. Publications
15800 NW 48th Avenue
Miami, Florida 33014

ISBN 0-87487-760-1

CONTENTS

INTRODUCCION

These Scandinavian folk songs are arranged for string orchestra (and piano) but can be used with violin groups or string quartet.

The third violin part is the same as the viola part.

I have added two instrumental folk melodies used frequently by Scandinavian folk musicians and played in the "bushes" without any accompaniment. I tried to reach a genuine folklore feeling in these pieces.

To reach the right "jazzy" feeling in "Nå Skiner Sola" and "Gammal Fäbodpsalm," I recommend that the piano accompaniment be used whenever possible.

Thanks to my friend, Anders Svenningsson, for his ideas in the piano parts for "Det var en Lördagsafton" and "Nå Skiner Sola."

THE SONGS

"Det var en Lördagsafton" is about a lovers' meeting; he is waiting for her on a Saturday evening, but she never comes even though she promised to. He cries out his disappointment: "I picked up wild roses, I'll never do it again / I loved you so dearly, I'll never love again."

In "Pigen Synger," a young girl is dreaming and singing: "It is true that there are lots of beautiful flowers in the summer garden, / But one of the roses is in a class by itself; her love to him!"

"Ack Värmeland, du Sköna" is about attachment to one's homeland: "Its valleys and forests give me a peace of silence, / And the wild waters sing their delightful song. / Here I want to live, here I want to die."

In "Nå Skiner Sola," a snowman is slowly melting away. On one hand we feel sorrow for the snowman disappearing and on the other hand joy and happiness for the onset of spring.

"On Neidolla Punapaula" tells of a girl dancing with the love of her life and tying a ribbon around his wrist so tightly that he can't run away!

In "Emma," the title character promises to be faithful, but she lets her fiancé down and then wants to keep the earrings he gave her.

"Ringnesen" is a typical Scandinavian folk dance tune.

"Gammal Fäbodpsalm," a hymn, is often played at Swedish funerals.

"Äppelbo Gånglåt" is often played at Swedish weddings.

INTRODUCCION

Estas piezas folklóricas escandinavas, arregladas para orquesta de cuerdas (y piano), también pueden usarse para cuarteto de cuerdas y grupos de violín.

La tercera parte de violín iguala a la parte de viola.

He añadido dos melodías folklóricas instrumentales usadas frecuentemente por músicos de folklore escandinavo y tocadas entre los "arbustos" sin ningún acompañamiento. Intenté alcanzar un sentimiento folklórico genuino en estas dos piezas.

Para lograr el sentimiento apropiado de "jazz" en "Nå Skiner Sola" y "Gammal Fäbodpsalm," recomiendo usar el acompañamiento de piano cada vez que sea posible.

Agradezco a mi amigo Anders Svenningsson sus ideas para las partes de piano de "Det var en Lördagsafton" y "Nå Skiner Sola."

LAS CANCIONES

"Det var en Lördagsafton" trata acerca de un encuentro amoroso; él la está esperando el sábado en la noche, pero ella nunca llega, aunque lo había prometido. El grita desilusionado: "Recogí rosas silvestres, no haré eso nunca más / Te amé tanto, nunca más amaré nuevamente."

En "Pigen Synger" una jovencita está cantando y soñando: "Es cierto que hay muchas flores hermosas en el jardín de verano, / pero una de las rosas está en su propio género: ¡su amor por él!"

"Ack Värmeland, du Sköna" trata sobre el amor a la Patria: "Sus valles y bosques me dan la paz del silencio, / y las aguas bravas cantan su encantadora canción: / Aquí quiero vivir, aquí quiero morir."

En "Nå Skiner Sola" un muñeco de nieve se está derritiendo poco a poco. Por una parte sentimos tristeza porque el muñeco de nieve está desapareciendo y por la otra, hay júbilo y alegría por la llegada de la primavera.

"On Neidolla Punapaula" narra cómo una muchacha que está bailando con el amor de su vida y está atando una cinta alrededor de la muñeca del muchacho con tanta fuerza ¡que éste no puede escaparse!

En "Emma," la protagonista le promete fidelidad a su futuro esposo; pero ella lo defrauda y sólo quiere quedarse con los zarcillos que él le regaló.

"Ringnesen" es una típica pieza de baile escandinavo.

"Gammal Fäbodpsalm," un himno, se toca a menudo en los funerales suecos.

"Äppelbo Gånglåt" se toca a menudo en las bodas suecas.

INTRODUCTION

Ces chansons folkloriques scandinaves sont arrangées pour un orchestre à cordes (et piano). Cependant, elles peuvent aussi être interprétées par un quatuor à cordes et violon groupe.

Le troisième violon correspond à la partie de l'alto.

J'ai inclu deux mélodies folkloriques instrumentales utilisées fréquemment par les musiciens folklorique scandinaves et jouées dans la 'brousse' sans aucun accompagnement. J'ai essayé d'obtenir une vraie expression folklorique dans ces deux morceaux.

Pour achever la vraie sensation du "jazz" dans "Nå Skiner Sola" et "Gammal Fäbodpsalm," je recommande qu'on utilize l'accompaniement au piano autant que possible.

Mes remerciements á mon ami, Anders Svenningsson, pour ses idees au piano pour la partie de "Det var en Lördagsafton" et "Nå Skiner Sola."

LES CHANSONS

"Det var en Lördagsafton." Un homme attend son amour un samedi soir, mais elle ne viendra pas, bien qu'elle le lui a promis. Il crit sa déception: "J'ai cueilli des roses sauvages, Je ne ferai plus jamais cela. / Je t'ai aimé tendrement, je n'aimerai plus jamais."

"Pigen Synger." Une jeune fille rêve et chante: "Est-il vrai vrai qu'il y a beaucoup de belles fleurs dans un jardin d'été, / mais une de ces roses est unique, son amour pour lui!"

"Ack Värmeland, du Sköna" parle de l'amour de son pays: "Ces vallées et forêts me donnent la paix du silence, / et les eaux agitées chantent leur chant ravissant. / Ici je veux vivre, ici je veux mourir."

"Nå Skiner Sola," un bonhomme de neige fond lentement. Il y a de la tristesse parceque le bonhomme de neige est en train de disparaître, nais aussi de la joie et du bonheur car le printemps arrive!

"On Neidolla Punapaula." Une fille danse avec l'amour de sa vie et noue un ruban autour de son poignet et le serre tres fort pour qu'il ne puisse s'échapper!

"Emma." Elle avait promis d'être fidèle, mais elle n'a pas tenu cette promesse à son fiancé; elle veut tout simplement garder les boucles d'oreille qu'il lui avait donné.

"Ringnesen." Une chanson folklorique typiquement scandinave pour la danse.

"Gammal Fäbodpsalm," un hymne, ce morceau est souvent joué dans les funerailles suédoises.

"Äppelbo Gånglåt" ce morceau est souvent joué dans les noces suédoises.

EINFÜHRUNG

Diese Skandinavischen Volkslieder wurden für ein Streichorchester (und Klavier) arrangiert, können aber auch für ein Streichquartett oder Violinengruppen benutzt werden.

Der dritte Geigenteil entspricht dem Bratschenteil.

Ich habe zwei instrumentale Volksmelodien hinzugefügt, die oft von skandinavischen Folkloremusikern benutzt werden und oft auch auf dem Land ohne Begleitung gespielt werden. Ich habe versucht, eine echte Folklorestimmung in die beiden Stücke einfließen zu lassen.

So dass man das richtige Gefühl im "Nå Skiner Sola" und "Gammal Fäbodpsalm" erreichen kann, empfehle ich, dass wenn möglich die Klavierbegleitung benutzt würde.

Herzlichen Dank zu meinem Freund, Anders Svenningsson, für seine Ideen in dem Klavierbegleitung von "Det var en Lördagsafton" und "Nå Skiner Sola."

DIESE LIEDER

"Det var en Lördagsafton." Ein Mann wartet auf seine Geliebte an einem Samstag abend, aber sie kommt nicht, obwohl sie es versprochen hatte. Er weint aus Enttäuschung: "Ich hatte wilde Rosen gepflückt, das mache ich nie wieder. / Ich liebte Dich so sehr, ich werde nie wieder jemanden lieben."

"Pigen Synger." Ein junges Mädchen träumt und singt: Es ist wahr, daß viele wunderschöne Blumen in dem Sommergarten blühen, / aber eine der Rosen ist in einer Klasse für sich, ihre Liebe zu ihm!"

"Ack Värmeland, du Sköna" ist über die Liebe für's Heimatland: "Seine Täler und Wälder geben mir den Frieden der Stille, / und die wilden Flüsse singen ihr liebliches Lied. / Hier möchte ich leben, hier möchte ich sterben."

"Nå Skiner Sola." Ein Schneemann schmilzt langsam. Man ist traurig, weil der Schneemann verschwindet, aber man freut sich und ist glücklich weil der Frühling kommt!

"On Neidolla Punapaula." Ein Mädchen tanzt mit der Liebe ihres Lebens und bindet ein Band ganz eng um sein Hand so daß er nicht weglaufen kann.

"Emma." Sie versprach treu zu sein, aber enttäuschte ihren Verlobten und will nur die Ohrringe behalten, die er ihr geschenkt hat.

"Ringnesen." Ein typischer skandinavischer Folkoretanz.

"Gammal Fäbodpsalm," eine Hymne, wird oft bei schwedischen Beerdigungen gespielt.

"Äppelbo Gånglåt" wird oft bei schwedischen Hochzeiten gespielt!

INTRODUZIONE

Queste canzoni popolari sono state arrangiate per essere eseguite da un'orchestra a corde (e pianoforte) ma possono anche essere interpretate da un quartetto d'archi e gruppi di violini.

La parte del terzo violino corrisponde alla viola.

Ho aggiunto due melodie folcloristiche strumentali usate frequentemente da musicisti Scandinavi e suonate nella "Macchia" senza alcun accompagnamento. In questi due pezzi ho cercato di dare una sensazione di folclore genuino.

Per raggiungere la giusta sensazione "jazzy" in "Nå Skiner Sola" e "Gammal Fäbodpsalm," raccomando se possibile di usare l'accompagnamento per piano.

Ringraziamenti al mio amico Anders Svenningsson per le sue idee nelle parti di piano in "Det var en Lördagsafton" e "Nå Skiner Sola."

LE CANZONI

"Det var en Lördagsafton." Un uomo attende la sua innamorata un Sabato sera, ma lei non si farà vedere malgrado lo avesse promesso. Lui piange la sua delusione: "Ho colto rose selvatiche, non lo farò mai più. / Ti ho amata così teneramente, non amerò mai più."

"Pigen Synger." Una giovane ragazza sta sognando e cantando: "É vero che ci sono molti bei fiori in un giardino estivo, / ma una delle rose è di una classe unica, il suo amore per lui!"

"Ack Värmeland, du Sköna." parla dell'amore per la propria patria: "Le sue valli e foreste mi danno la pace del silenzio, / e le acque turbolenti cantano la loro incantevole canzone. / Qui voglio vivere, qui voglio morire."

"Nå Skiner Sola," Un pupazzo di neve si sta sciogliendo lentamente. C'è tristezza perché il pupazzo sta scomparendo, ma c'è anche gioia e felicità per l'arrivo della primavera!

"On Neidolla Punapaula." Una ragazza balla con l'amore della sua vita e lega un nastro al suo polso, molto stretto per impedirgli di scappare via!

"Emma." Lei promise di essere fedele, ma invece lo abbandonò e vuole solo tenersi gli orecchini che lui le donò.

"Ringnesen." Una tipica canzone popolare Scandinava da ballare.

"Gammal Fäbodpsalm," un inno, suonato spesso nei funerali Scandinavi.

"Äppelbo Gånglåt" suonata spesso nei matrimoni Scandinavi!

ACK VÄRMELAND, DU SKÖNA
(SWEDEN)
(Oh Beautiful Värmeland)

PIGEN SYNGER (DENMARK)
(Singing Girl)

CELLO

Traditional
Arranged by KITTY PÄÄKKÖNEN

Maestoso (♩ = 88-92)

DET VAR EN LØRDAG AFTEN
(DENMARK)
(One Saturday Evening)

CELLO

Traditional
Arranged by KITTY PÄÄKKÖNEN

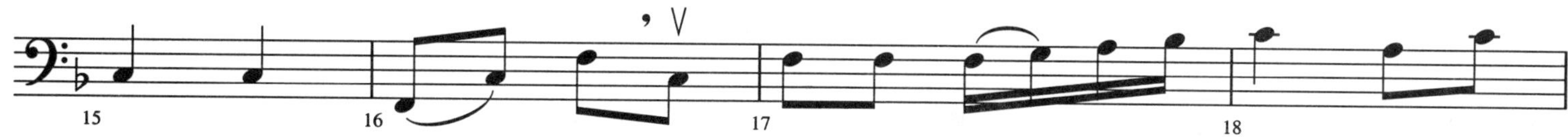

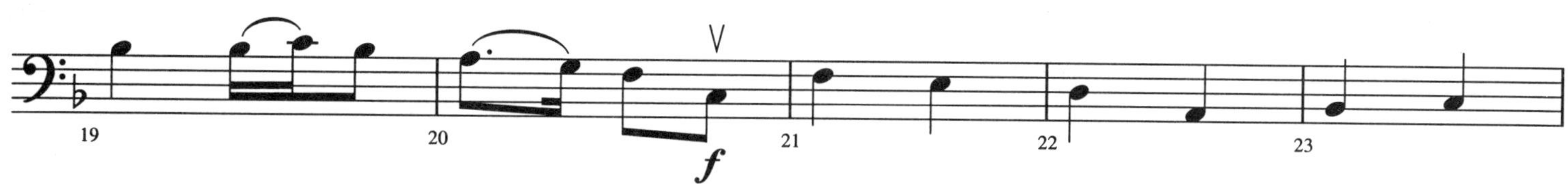

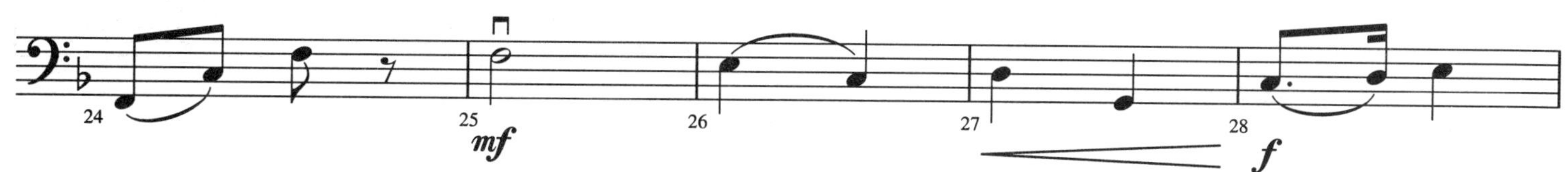

RINGNESEN (NORWAY)

(A Round Game)

NÅ SKINER SOLA (NORWAY)
(Now the Sun is Shining)

CELLO

EMMA (FINLAND)

CELLO

Traditional
Arranged by KITTY PÄÄKKÖNEN

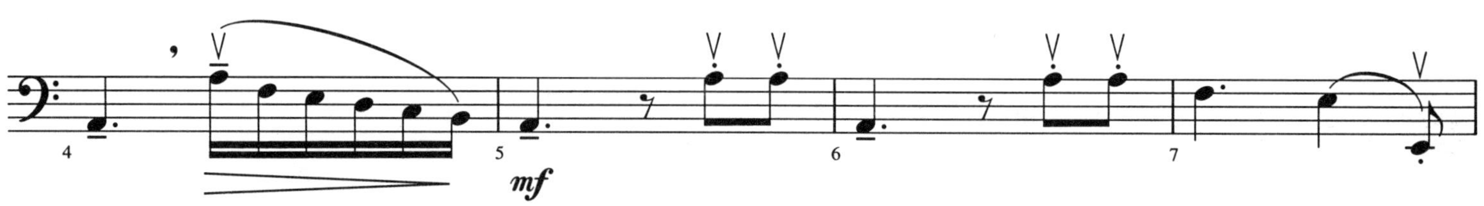

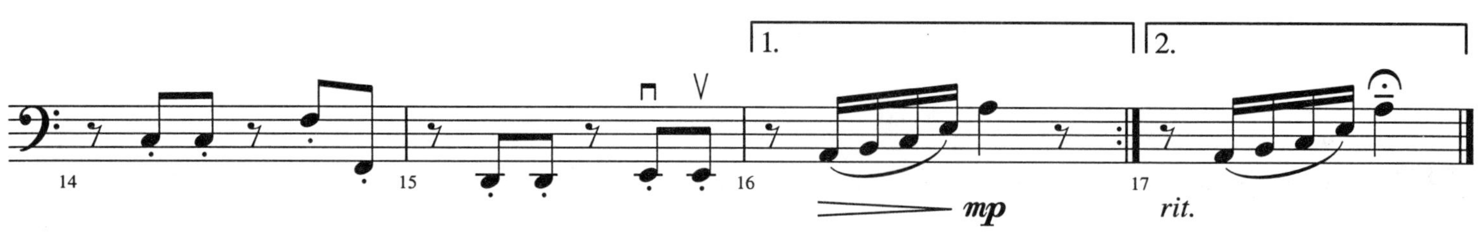

ON NEIDOLLA PUNAPAULA
(SWEDEN and FINLAND)
(The Young Girl With Red Ribbons)

GAMMAL FÄBODPSALM
(Old Chalet Hymn)

CELLO

Traditional
Arranged by OSKAR LINDBERG

ÄPPELBO GÅNGLÅT (SWEDEN)
(Applenest Walking Tune)

The *Strings Around the World* series is designed for student string orchestras, string quartets, or violin groups. The arrangements are not technically difficult, but some contain rhythmic challenges for fun and training, which are easily worked out in rehearsals. The rhythmic and tonal variations of these folk songs provide enjoyment to performers and audiences alike.

FOLK SONGS OF
AUSTRALIA

arranged by Lois Shepheard

Titles are: Barn Dance (Australian Folk Song) • The Black Velvet Band (Australian Folk Song) • Botany Bay (Australian Folk Song) • Brisbane Ladies (Australian Folk Song) • Click Go the Shears (Australian Folk Song) • Jim Jones at Botany Bay (Australian Folk Song) • Kookaburra (Sinclair) • Along the Road to Gundagai (O'Hagan) • A Thousand Miles Away (Australian Folk Song) • Waltzing Matilda (Cowan).

(0782) Score
(0783) Violin 1
(0784) Violin 2
(0788) Violin 3
(0785) Viola
(0786) Cello
(0787) Bass

FOLK SONGS OF THE
U.S.A.

arranged by William Starr

Titles are: Billy Barlowe • Buffalo Gals • Go Down Moses • Home on the Range • Jim Along Josie • Joshua Fit de Battle of Jericho • Oh Susanna • Old Joe Clark • Sweet Betsy from Pike.

(0796) Score
(0797) Violin 1
(0798) Violin 2
(0956) Violin 3
(0799) Viola
(0838) Cello
(0839) String Bass

FOLK SONGS OF
SCANDINAVIA

(Folk Songs from Denmark, Finland, Norway, and Sweden)
arranged by Kitty Pääkkönen

Titles are: Ack Värmeland, du Sköna (Sweden) • Pigen Synger (Denmark) • Det var en Lördagsafton (Denmark) • Ringnesen (Norway) • Nå Skiner Sola (Norway) • Emma (Finland) • On Neidolla Punapaula (Finland) • Gammal Fäbodpsalm (Sweden) • Äppelbo Gånglåt (Sweden).

(0756) Score
(0757) Violin 1
(0758) Violin 2
(0766) Violin 3
(0759) Viola
(0760) Cello
(0765) Bass